God's Birth

Announcements

Our world has not been the same

since God delivered these

Birth Announcements

Rev. Stephen R. Crowell, M.div

With Lee E. Capodagli

God's Birth Announcements

Reverend Stephen R. Crowell, Mdiv
With Lee E. Capodagli

© 2011 by Wave Dancer Productions
Rushford, New York

Printed in the United States

Produced by Wave Dancer Productions
Post Office Box 64
Rushford, NY 14777

If you have any questions or comments concerning this book please contact the Rev. Crowell at pastor@konxions.org.

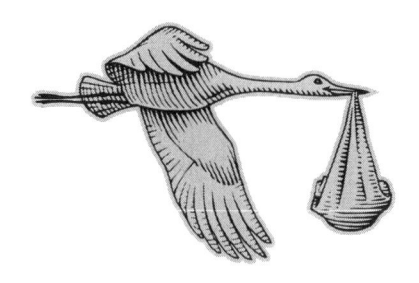

Table of Contents

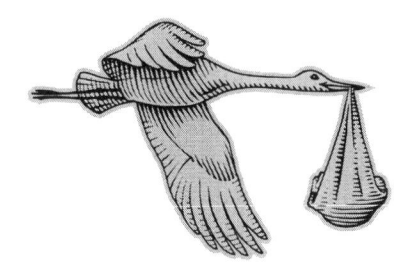

Acknowledgements

Ministry has become a joy for me since I have partnered with so many different individuals. God has given each of them outstanding talents. I am amazed in the different ways in which God breaks through each week as we come together making preparations for each service.

I am so thankful for my wife Kristan. Without her talents and her care for me I would never have the courage to step out into this world. She encourages me, supports me and is willing to hold my feet to the fire. This is no easy task and she has grown into to this task extremely well.

Pastor Craig Buelow has become an extremely important part of my ministry puzzle. If Kristan is the four corners, then Craig has begun to fill in the rest of the border. Daily Craig and I talk about sermons, services, congregants, visionary plans, and how we each are growing into our ministry.

Recently Lee Capodagli has joined the team and is also helping Craig to place pieces of the ministry puzzle in place. The final picture is becoming clearer. Lee brings a fresh perspective and creativity to our ministry. Each day that we work together I continually see the world from a different perspective. I have told Lee that he has joined the "Tether Team." I need people to help hold me in place till the appropriate time for release.

The members of the ministry team that go week in and week out without much recognition are those who participate in the services or in those chance meetings during the week. Each individual that we minister has an important role in providing a ministry to us as well. The team and I love to learn about God and the love God has for the world through those whom God has placed in our path.

Lastly I want to lift up my parents who have given me a lifelong model on how to do this thing we call ministry. Mom, Betty Crowell, has always seen the lighter side. When I was young I remember her having charge of the Sunday evening service. She would take the latest game show and turn into an activity where God was praised. My father, Nelson Crowell, is one of the best speakers I have ever heard. He taught the scriptures in such a way that fidgety teenagers would sit up and listen. He also taught me how to love people and how to shepherd them continuously towards the kingdom of God.

With God's Grace I wish to thank all of you for your participation in my life and in my ministry. Together let us find the heart of God and desire to bring as many individuals to the witness the birth of Jesus.

I also feel that I need to express my appreciation to the Triune God. Many times as I was typing out a sentence that held a certain point that I wanted to get across, it seemed that words and sentences would just poor out me that I had no clue where they came from. I pray that many sections of this book are truly inspired for your reading. I know that I learned much this time around.

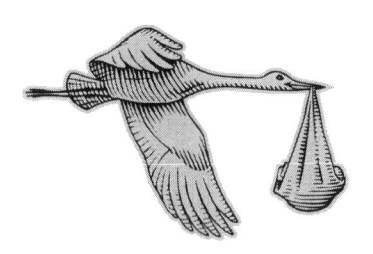

Foreword

In our North American culture we love to celebrate life changing events. Each one of these milestones offers the opportunity to send out an announcement to friends and relatives. Examples of these events or milestones are graduations from school, the first job or a new job, weddings, anniversaries, and retirement parties.

Each of these life changing events would never happen without the first announcement, a Birth Announcement. These proud announcements always change our world in the most dramatic ways. Especially for the mother who will carry their child for nearly a year, but who will also hold that child in her heart for a lifetime. These Birth Announcements let everyone know that each child has a role to play, part of God's ordained and ordered world.

Between my wife and I we have had seven awesome opportunities to share with our closest friends and family the news of our impeding children's births. I was the one that could never hold the secret. I had to share with the whole world our news.

Each time I wanted to shout from the nearest mountain top. Everyone needed to share in the joy that I had in deep in my soul. I wanted to prepare fthem for the upcoming birth so they would be just as excited as I was.

I can watch over and over again the scene in the Disney's movie "Lion King" where the father lifts up his lion cub for the first time in front of the Pride. You can almost feel his heart pounding so hard that it just may burst through his chest cage. If I had a Pride all seven of my children would have been held up for all to see. As it were I spent a lot of time contacting everyone to let them know of the good, no, great news of another child being born into the Crowell Family.

Recently I was reading an article by Tim Townsend, a religion reporter for the Post-Dispatch. In this particular article for the STLtoday.com he concentrated on greeting cards, which incidentally was a 7.5 billion industry in 2010. The Javits Center in New York in May of 2011was the site of the National Stationary Show. In this one place eleven thousand buyers converged on nine hundred venders.

Kelly Bristol who is part of the Greeting Card Association acknowledged that the wedding cards and supplies have the largest sales. The second most popular seller was the sale of birth announcements. Bristol went on to say that birth announcements are the venue for which people can celebrate life.

Tim Townsend shares with his readers that the greeting card industry has only been making these timely announcements for a little more than a century. Tim goes on to write that the tradition announcing births has gone on for millennia. He is quick to point out that at the time of Jesus being born the announcement came through stars and angels instead of through the postal service.

Townsend also made a great observation that two of the announcements were before the birth where Mary and Joseph learned of their incredible future. Two announcements were for the Shepherds and Magi after the birth that saw signs and wonders in the night sky. Just as in any birth announcement, Tim Townsend wrote that the baby's name was just as important then as it is now.

Mary was visited by the angel Gabriel with instructions to name him Jesus.

"God's Birth Announcements" examines how God made the ultimate birth announcement to the world. Just as I was excited to share my announcement to the world, so was our Creator God. God, the Father, imbedded small little announcements in the writings of the Old Testament. In fact, many authors and pastors believe that all of the Old Testament is a story to lead the reader to the birth of Jesus. The Trinity had a plan for the redemption of the world through the sacrifice of Jesus on the cross and the miracle of Christ's resurrection from the grave.

Our original designer, our Lord God, placed in the Old Testament bread crumbs to lead the Israelites towards the coming birth of God's son, Jesus our Christ (Savior & Messiah). For example the prophet Isaiah spoke of a child to be born, a child who will offer peace to the descendants of King David.

This child will have a kingdom that will uphold justice and right living forever. The child's name will be Mighty God, Prince of Peace and Wonderful Counselor. Jesus is the fulfillment of these ancient words. He did not come to fulfill them in an earthly kingdom, but in a spiritual kingdom. (see "A Prayer for Common People"[1] for a deeper explanation.)

In **"God's Birth Announcements"** we will examine how God used the prophets to announce the coming 'king,' how the angels were used to announce to both Joseph and Mary the birth of their son, the 'king,' how both the shepherds and the magi made public this announcement.

---

[1] Stephen Crowell. 2011. A Prayer for a Common Person. Wave Dancer Productions. (Available through popular media outlets)

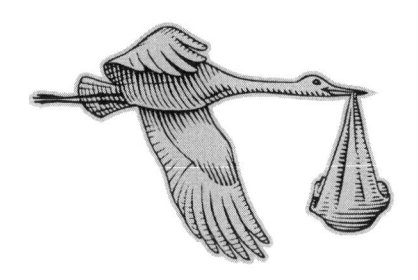

The First Announcement

God's Announcement to the Israelites

Where does one begin when looking for the Birth Announcement for the Son of God? Has it become possible that many today couldn't answer that question even though in one form or another each year we have celebrated the birth of Jesus our Christ? It seems that we have lost the spiritual and historical meaning of Christmas.

Once upon a time, we looked forward to our extended families getting together. Children and grandchildren would descend upon the ancestral family home. Together they would bundle up with coats, hats, mufflers, and mittens to walk to Community Christmas Eve service. This became for many the way in which God handed out the

Birth Announcement for the arrival of the baby Jesus.

Instead, merchants capitalize on the giving frenzy that surrounds the 'Holiday Season.' They have begun to display their 'Seasonal' items along with the Halloween costumes and candy. Sales clerks and customer service representatives hand out a warm "Happy Holidays" instead of a wide smile with "Merry Christmas" on their lips.

God's Birth Announcement to the world didn't begin in our present day Christmas Eve services or in our local church. Instead, God has placed a bread crumb trail that leads to Christ's arrival throughout the Old Testament. God in small little obscure ways has made it known that someday in a little out of the way place called Bethlehem God's son would be born. God's son would become the messiah for those who have been separated from their Creator.

What is a Messiah?

God's Birth Announcements are set in a very specific context in which we are to examine the hints, the bread crumbs, found in scripture that lead the readers towards the messiah. Messiah is actually a Hebrew word that is spelled "mashiah" (מָשִׁיחַ) which means "the anointed." In some scriptures this description has been expanded to include: "the anointed one" and "the anointed king."

Each of these written announcements are found embedded in the Old Testament. Some biblical scholars would say that all of the Old Testament scripture points to the Christian Messiah. This may or may not be true, but there are some scriptures that clearly direct the readers to a future messiah. The Old Testament contains three specific instances where individuals received an anointing.

The nineteenth chapter of First Kings illustrates three examples of just such an anointing. Elijah was commanded by the Lord to enter the wilderness of Damascus to anoint Hazael the **king** over Aram (vs. 15) and Nimshi as the Israelite **king** (vs. 16). The Lord also directed Elijah to anoint his successor Elisha the son of Shaphat as a **prophet** (vs. 19). In Exodus 28:41, Moses was commanded by the Lord to anoint Aaron and his sons so they could serve as **priests**.

The anointing of the young David in First Samuel illustrates well the power of an anointing by the Lord. In the sixteenth chapter the Lord rebukes Samuel in his grief over the rejection of Saul as the king of Israel. Samuel is ordered to fill a horn with oil and to set out for the house of Jesse. The Lord had chosen one of Jesse's sons to be the next king.

King Saul was at odds with God and if he knew that Samuel was about to anoint another as king, Samuel's life would have been at risk. Together, the Lord and Samuel put together a plan that would allow safe passage for Samuel to reach Bethlehem. Therefore, Samuel took a heifer with him for a sacrifice.

The elders of the city came out to meet with the prophet of the Lord full of fear and trembling. They wanted to know if Samuel came to them with a peaceful intent. Samuel assured them that he did. He simply had come to offer a sacrifice. After all of the town's leaders had been sanctified they were invited to participate in the sacrifice.

After the sacrifice, the Lord again directed Samuel to look over the sons of Jesse. Each one had an outer appearance of greatness. Yet, the Lord reminded Samuel to look only on the heart. Seven sons passed before Samuel and the Lord did not approve of these. Samuel asked Jesse if these were all of his sons. Jesse said the youngest still remained to come, but he was out tending the flock.

Samuel said they would sit and wait for the young boy to arrive. When Samuel saw David, he noticed his bright, beautiful eyes and his ruddy complexion. It was then that the Lord told Samuel to rise and anoint the boy.

Samuel took the horn filled with oil and poured it over the young David. Immediately the spirit of the Lord came in a very powerful way upon David. From that day forward this spirit remained with David. The scripture goes onto reveal that even as the spirit was entering David the spirit was also leaving King Saul. In fact, an evil spirit entered into Saul's heart to torment him.

When an individual is anointed in the Middle Eastern tradition that person traditionally is fully covered in scented oil. Dousing David's head was symbolic of this. This was an outward sign of an inward change. The spirit of the Lord covered David by indwelling in him. David had been given abilities beyond his normal capabilities.

This story of David helps us to more fully understand the anointing process which sets those serving the Lord apart for service. Priests, prophets and kings were anointed to serve the Lord in specific ways. Now, when reading the Old Testament, readers will notice the power that these individuals were able to bring to bear on the circumstance they encountered. These priests, prophets and kings were not acting upon the situation in their own strength, but with the power of the Lord God within them.

God's Birth Announcements direct our vision to a future messiah, to an anointed one. The Israelites were promised one that would come in the full power of an anointing—in other words, as king, prophet and priest, to fulfill the plan of salvation for God's chosen people and also for the gentiles. Christians derive their very name from the one that was set aside to save the world as the ultimate sacrifice. Some of the other names in the Old Testament for the coming anointed king are: Immanuel (God with us); Wonderful Counselor; King of kings; and Messiah.

Today we call out to the name of Jesus Christ. Many would believe that Christ is merely Jesus' last name. In actuality the word "messiah" (anointed) is translated from the Hebrew into the Greek, Christos. We have translated the Greek Christos into the English form as the Christ. Jesus has become for us the anointed one. Jesus was covered with the anointing of the Spirit of the Lord when he was baptized by John. Jesus for the Christian becomes the fulfillment of the Old Testament prophecies.

Why is there a need for a Messiah?

This has been a question asked throughout the ages, so--why *do* we need to be saved? What do we need to be saved *from*? One may say: "I live a life that is honorable. I am better than *those* people." The truth is that each one of us is in need of being saved from our own selfish character. We may be good, but we are not perfect. The question is also based on ones perspective. When looking over our lives we tend to gloss over the times that we have fallen short of even our self-proposed ethical standard.

Speaking of standards and perspectives, who among us gets to chose what is good or bad, right from wrong? Each one of us has our own personal agenda and goals. We all come from different backgrounds with different standards. In the end we all have a selfish character that can only see life from our own particular perspective.

Let us look at this issue of standards from the view point of the creator. This world we live in is not of our own doing, but of God's. So, it would seem logical that a creating God would feel legitimate in setting the standards of creation.

Examine as an illustration a ceramic pitcher used in the ceremony at a baptism. The ceramic pitcher doesn't tell the potter how to make its shape.

The creator, or potter, has full license to mold, shape and color it according to the need of the one using it. The pitcher is simply a tool that is used to accomplish the holding of water that will be blessed.

The potter sets the standards--not the pitcher. It is the same with the creation of the world both seen and unseen. The God of creation knows the perfect needs of humanity. The God of creation has placed on the creation perfect standards that are to be followed. The problem arises when we, the ceramic pitcher, become so involved in daily living that we can only focus on the moment and not the larger picture.

It is from this narrow perspective that we try to make sense of what is around us and how we interact with others and with events. We forget that we were created to be a tool of the Creator God. He has a specific purpose for our lives. So when we begin to put forward our desires and our dreams they do not always line up with God's.

It is our character and our nature that causes our separation from God, our creator. Paul in Ephesians explains that the desires of our flesh are driven by our passions that cause us to be susceptible to the evil powers.

Ephesians 2:1-9 (NRSV) You were dead through the trespasses and sins in which you once lived, following the course of this world, following the ruler of the power of the air, the spirit that is now at work among those who are disobedient. All of us once lived among them in the passions of our flesh, following the desires of flesh and senses, and we were by nature children of wrath, like everyone else. But God, who is rich in mercy, out of the great love with which he loved us even when we were dead through our trespasses, made us alive together with Christ--by grace you have been saved--and raised us up with him and seated us with him in the heavenly places in Christ Jesus, so that in the ages to come he might show the immeasurable riches of his grace in kindness toward us in Christ Jesus. For by grace you have been saved through faith, and this is not your own doing; it is the gift of God--not the result of works, so that no one may boast.

Why do we need a messiah? It is because in our own desires we will almost always choose those things that only fulfill our needs. It is those choices that keep us separated for the blessing of God who truly loves us. We need a God who will override our character. We need a God that looks beyond our faults and our inabilities. We need one who would stand in our place or would be our sacrifice.

What are the Bread Crumbs for a Messiah?

God began to give clues to what was to come concerning the birth of the Anointed One that would become for the entire world a Savior. The Creator God, the Father of all chose to place these small birth announcements throughout the writings of the Old Testament. These birth announcements were like bread crumbs leading those who were searching for the coming event that was to take place in Bethlehem--the birth of Jesus.

These bread crumbs give clues to those who were looking so that they would understand the deity of Jesus, they would know the place of his birth, they would be able to trace the lineage from which he would be born, and they would even be able to discern the character of the one that would give him birth.

The Messiah would be the Lord God

Isa 9:6 & 7 (NRSV) For a child has been born for us, a son given to us; authority rests upon his shoulders; and he is named <u>Wonderful Counselor, Mighty God, Everlasting Father, Prince of Peace.</u> His authority shall grow continually, and there shall be endless peace for the throne of David and his kingdom. He will establish and uphold it with justice and with righteousness from this time onward and forevermore. The zeal of the LORD of hosts will do this.

Psalms 2:7 I will tell of the decree of the LORD: He said to me, "You are my son; today I have begotten you.

The prophet Isaiah predicted the coming of a ruler. Jesus has become for us the eternal ruler that provides for us an everlasting peace. We sing each year for peace on earth, yet the peace is not coming in the form of peace as in avoidance of conflict among people and nations, but through the peace found in one's spirit.

This peace we seek for comes from a kingdom that is based on justice and right living. The peace is given to us because the kingdom will last forever.

Bread Crumbs Reveal The Messiah:

Isaiah 9:1 (NRSV) But there will be no gloom for those who were in anguish. In the former time he brought into contempt the land of Zebulun and the land of Naphtali, but in the latter time he will make glorious the way of the sea, the land beyond the Jordan, Galilee of the nations.

Jesus was the son of a carpenter that lived in Nazareth, a town near the Sea of Galilee.

Genesis 49:10 (NRSV) The scepter shall not depart from Judah, nor the ruler's staff from between his feet, until tribute comes to him; and the obedience of the peoples is his.

Micah 5:2 (NRSV) But you, O Bethlehem of Ephrathah, who are one of the little clans of Judah, from you shall come forth for me one who is to rule in Israel, whose origin is from of old, from ancient days.

Matthew 2:1-6 (NRSV) In the time of King Herod, after Jesus was born in Bethlehem of Judea, wise men from the East came to Jerusalem, asking, "Where is the child who has been born king of the Jews? For we observed his star at its rising, and have come to pay him homage." When King Herod heard this, he was frightened, and all Jerusalem with him; and calling together all the chief priests and scribes of the people, he inquired of them where the Messiah was to be born. They told him, "In Bethlehem of Judea; for so it has been written by the prophet: 'And you, Bethlehem, in the land of Judah, are by no means least among the rulers of Judah; for from you shall come a ruler who is to shepherd my people Israel.'"

"O Little Town of Bethlehem" is one of my favorite songs to sing throughout the year. It is here that history has been played out. On these deserted slopes there once was a little boy named David who tended sheep for his father. David was later anointed in the village by the prophet Samuel to be the king over the Israelites. It only stands to reason that God would use this site for the birth of the ultimate king of the Israelites. Just as David was the last to be picked because of his humble status in life, Jesus was born in a humble stable. It may seem incredible, but it may be possible, perhaps even likely, that the same sheep that quietly grazed the hills around Bethlehem looked upon the birth of *both* of these kings.

The Messiah would come from the line of David

Jeremiah 23:4-6 (NRSV) I will raise up shepherds over them who will shepherd them, and they shall not fear any longer, or be dismayed, nor shall any be missing, says the LORD. The days are surely coming, says the LORD, when I will raise up for David a righteous Branch, and he shall reign as king and deal wisely, and shall execute justice and righteousness in the land. In his days Judah will be saved and Israel will live in safety. And this is the name by which he will be called: "The LORD is our righteousness."

Isaiah 11:10 (NRSV) On that day the root of Jesse shall stand as a signal to the peoples; the nations shall inquire of him, and his dwelling shall be glorious.

God had made a promise to King David that someone out of his lineage would continue to rule over Israel. In Matthew's genealogies Jesus the Messiah is in the line of King David, the son of Jesse. When Caesar needed to know the size of his kingdom he sent out a decree that all of his subjects would go to their ancestral home. Therefore, through this action Joseph and Mary left Nazareth to go to the little town of Bethlehem where Mary gave birth to the Son of God. Here again the prophecies were fulfilled.

The Messiah would come from a Virgin

Isaiah 7:13 & 14 (NRSV) Then Isaiah said: "Hear then, O house of David! Is it too little for you to weary mortals, that you weary my God also? Therefore the Lord himself will give you a sign. Look, the young woman is with child and shall bear a son, and shall name him Immanuel.

God, the father of Jesus, has offered his son to us as a replacement for our character or our sinful nature. Jesus, the anointed one, has become for us our savior. It is through Jesus that we can now live in a close relationship with God the Father – our Creator.

God loved us so much that a plan, a provision, was made for each one of us to be forgiven from our sins. Out of this love, God provided a trail of bread crumbs for us. This trail pointed to the birth of his son, Jesus. It is this trail that we can look back to over time and space that proves to us that this was a preplanned event.

 # Saturday

Please use this Space to record any special notes that you thought of while you read this section.

Monday

"What is a Messiah?"

What is the importance of understanding what a Messiah is? Why do we need to know?

Is it important to know (understand) that a Messiah may be found in kings, prophets and priests within the Old Testament?

In looking at the New Testament where do you see that Jesus fulfils all three of these roles?

 # Tuesday

"Why Is There a Need For a Messiah?"

How do you feel about God (the potter) shaping and forming you (the pot) without you having any control over the shaping process?

Does this give you a sense of freedom in who you are, or do you bristle (feel like a slave) because you feel you have no freedom (don't have any input in the process)?

If God has created our base character, what causes the (our) separation from God? Is it seeing our character in the light of God's view, or is it in the light of our own personal view?

 # Wednesday

"The Messiah Would Be The Lord God"

Re-read Isaiah Chapter Nine. What do those names mean to you? [Wonderful Counselor, etc.]

If God is saying there will be peace under his authority, why do we have no peace in the world today?

What did Jesus say about the kingdom of God? Is it a political peace or is it a peace of soul?

 **Thursday**

"The Messiah Would Come From The Line of David"

The Old Testament is full of god's promises. What is the promise/covenant given to Abraham?

In God's plan, what is the plan for the Hebrew children to the rest of the people in the world?

At what point do they fulfill, in total, their mission to the gentiles?

God again makes a promise with King David that it is thru his line the ultimate Anointed One would be found. How does this answer the previous question?

 **Friday**

"The Messiah Would Come From a Virgin"

Isaiah must have become frustrated with his fellow travelers. What does the word "weary" conjure up for you? If Isaiah is using the word in a negative sense towards his fellow mortals, how does that reveal what he thinks of their opinion of God (pestering Him—"wearying" Him—constantly)?

If the Israelites failed to perceive the signs preceding the Virgin birth, are we today also failing to see the signs of that birth? If so—how?

The Second Announcement

The Angels' Announcement to Mary

Luke 1:26-38

The young hand maiden named Mary must have had some regular everyday normal dreams that carried her through life. Dreams that every young girl who was pledged to be married must have dreamed; what it would be like to have a husband and even her own house to manage. She would have dreamed of growing old with Joseph and having a family with him. What she never dreamed was that she would be the fulfillment of all of God's Birth Announcements.

Mary never dreamed that she would one day see an angel named Gabriel, a messenger, sent by the King of kings, the Lord of all, and the Creator of all that is seen and unseen. Yet, this exactly is what happened to this lowly young girl of nearly sixteen years. God had dreamed bigger dreams for Mary and had sent her a special invitation to participate. She was now being asked to dream bigger dreams than she could have ever imagined.

God's Birth Announcement that was given to Mary certainly altered her dream of a simple family that would live out a simple life living in a simple town called Nazareth. Mary was now being called out of her simple life, called out by God, called to rise above her daily routine and her simple dreams to lead a different life with a higher calling.

The Angel's Announcement

In the first chapter of Luke the angel Gabriel, the chief messenger from God, came to Mary with a startling announcement. "Greetings you are have found favor with God. The Lord your God is with you." Mary, being immersed in her daily routine, must have been very shocked to have this messenger of God physically enter her home.

In fact, Luke says that she was perplexed by the extraordinary words being spoken to her. Just as an earthquake shakes the ground, Mary's world was now trembling and moving under her feet. These words from God would forever change the course of her life. Mary, a simple servant girl, is being addressed by God's messenger. She is being told that she has been lifted up to a special place in God's kingdom.

Mary spent some moments, fleeting as they may have seemed, to contemplate what had just been said to her. "What sort of greeting is this when someone announces that you have found favor in the sight of God?" While she had these thoughts going through her head Gabriel again reaffirmed to her that she had found favor with God.

In Gabriel's message to Mary, she was called "O favored one." This was essentially the same affirmation that both Moses (Gen. 6-8) and Abraham (Gen. 17:5-8) had received from the Lord. They too had been highly favored in the sight of God. Mary would have known that in her day that this message, or statement, would have been translated to mean; God's Holy Grace is on you. This pronouncement would have placed Mary in a very small, very select group of biblical figures so honored by God.

Mary Ponders the Announcement

Mary may have been a lowly teenage girl that lived in a town of about fifty families, but she wasn't unintelligent. As Mary was hearing the news that was being given to her she began to ponder on the full implications that would come with this, God's Birth Announcement. Fear must have been welling up in her thoughts because Gabriel offered her hope in telling her not to be afraid.

I had often read this passage and merely thought that the angel Gabriel was telling her not to be afraid of his presence. Instead, this messenger of God was letting Mary know that she should not be afraid for herself or for her child's future. The Son of the Most High would be formed in her womb. Her son would sit on the throne of David and that the kingdom in which he would rule would last forever.

The fear that Mary felt was derived directly from the culture in which she lived. Luke points out in this historical document[2] Mary's position within the community. Luke felt it important to recognize that she was a virgin who was engaged to be married to Joseph. This is important to know, because in her village Mary being pregnant out of wedlock would have caused her to be vulnerable to vindictive judgments from those around her and subject to punishment under the Law.

Nazareth was an extremely small settlement of about fifty families with probably no more than five hundred people living in or near the village. Mary would have been known to each person in and around this rural hamlet. She would not have been able to escape their knowledge of her condition and the fact that she had become pregnant before her marriage to Joseph.

Marriage at this time was a complicated social dance. One must first be engaged or betrothed to another. This was done through a

[2] Luke was a doctor who traveled with the apostle Paul. Luke is the author of both Luke and Acts. It has been long considered that these two books were at one time one book and have since been broken apart. Luke explains in the first four verses of chapter one that many others had written their accounts of Jesus and the beginnings of the church, but he also felt the need to do his own research by going and doing personal interviews.

traditional matchmaking process. The engagement would have been just as binding as the marriage ceremony. The only way for this engagement to be broken would be to enact divorce proceedings.

In Joseph and Mary's day, just as today, it is expected that reasons will be given to break an engagement. If Joseph had followed through with a divorce then Mary would have been exposed to those in her town that she had conceived a child outside of marriage. Joseph would also be accusing her of having a sexual relationship with someone other than himself.

Mary knew that her pregnancy was scandalous to those with power, those in higher social classes and those with money. Men definitely dominated these societal circles. Within the Hebrew tradition women and girls were not looked upon favorably.

Mary knew that she was risking her life when she agreed to obey the will of her Lord. If she was rejected by Joseph, she would have broken the Jewish Law of not have sex before marriage. Therefore she would have had to face her accusers and be liable to stoning or other punishment for her sin. This may be one of the reasons she waited to tell her betrothed, Joseph, of her pregnancy.

Mathew's Gospel clearly indicates that Mary had been pregnant for some time before Joseph became aware of her condition. Could it be that she was afraid of what Joseph would do to her? We will never know for sure, but it seems reasonable that Mary's fear held her back from discussing this with him earlier.

If Mary had not been stoned then she would have faced the possibility of being rejected by her own family. She had a very real fear that she would have been cast out of their village or at the very least have been estranged. We learn more of this cultural tradition by what happens to the Samaritan woman in the Gospel of John. This woman, who had several husbands, also lived in a very small village. She could only go to the well during the heat of the day when no one else would be around. If she went early in the morning with the other women of the village she would have been teased or shunned with silence.

Have we not carried this shame into our own culture today? I know from first-hand experience that many young ladies in the past were escorted off to unfamiliar places to have their children in silence. My mother told me of a childhood friend that one day was absent from the community. She later learned that her parents sent her clear across the country to have a child. It was the hope that good upstanding families could be saved from public scrutiny and to avoid embarrassment.

Mary's Fear for Jesus as the Chief Prophet

Mary, as a young girl, grew up in a town that was the home of an off duty priest.[3] It was here in the streets and near the synagogue that Mary would have heard the priest talking concerning the prophets of old. Mary knew that well the stories of the prophet that had been murdered for speaking the truth. God had given to these prophets' announcements for the people of God to turn from their evil and sinful ways of living.

God's people knew that the truth they heard would change their lives and their habits. It would totally alter the way in which they lived. Mary knew from prophecy that her son, Jesus would be the greatest prophet to ever live. Jesus would be the chief of prophets. If she was not afraid for herself, she would have definitely been afraid for her unborn child.

---

[3] It was through her mother's side that Mary was related to her cousin Elizabeth. Elizabeth, the mother of John, was married to a priest that worked in the temple. We also have evidence that Nazareth was home to priest due to its root name being listed in I Chronicles 24:7-19.

Mary's fear was truly not that far afield. Jesus *did* die at the hands of many who could not understand the truth when it was presented to them. Jesus once told his disciples that he talked in parables because those around him couldn't understand the plain truth. Those people who didn't want to change their ways put the Son of God on the lowly tree meant for criminals.

Mary's Fear for Jesus as the King

It was through Gabriel, the messenger of God, that Mary learned that all the prophecies of a future savior would be fulfilled. It was her unborn child that would soon be the King of Kings and sit on David's throne, and her son's kingdom would last forever.

Even though Mary was young, she was aware of the political risk that faced her unborn child. Israel, as well as the known world, was under the control of the Roman Empire. Even in the small town of Nazareth that power could be felt. Nazareth was just a few miles away from one of the resort towns where political leaders and high ranking officers in the army went to rest and relax.

Mary's understood fully that God's Birth Announcement placed her unborn child at great risk. The Roman emperors were known to kill even members of their own family to maintain their power. Gabriel was standing there in front of her proclaiming that her son would be the king to sit on the ancient throne of King David. This news would place her son in direct conflict then with the current political powers.

Mary had good reason to fear for the political safety of her son. The Magi as they were looking for the new born king went looking in all the places a king should be born. They went to palace of King Herod, the ruler over the Jews. King Herod had also killed many in his own family to retain his seat on the throne. After learning about his competition he sent out a decree to murder all the baby boys in his region.

Mary must have had all of these fears and doubts running full speed through her mind as God's messenger was speaking to her. It was into her newly-shaken world that Gabriel brought this assurance: "Do not be afraid, Mary, for you have found favor with God." (Luke 1:30b NRSV) Mary knew that she would not be alone in this journey. She had been chosen to carry the son of God. She knew that God would go with her and would protect her from all that assailed her.

God's Birth Announcement

God concealed his son's birth announcements within the historic, prophetic and poetic books of the Old Testament that were given to the Jewish people. These Birth Announcements were sent out to everyone, but only to those who were seeking the messiah could receive and understand them.

Then when it was time for the messiah's birth the invitation list became extremely shortened, including only Mary and Joseph, the lowly shepherds and the magi.

With any birth announcement the name of the baby is the most important component found within the note. The angel Gabriel instructed Mary to name the child Jesus. This child, Jesus, became the savior of the world. It was Jesus who came to take away our actions that keep us separated from the Creator God. Jesus became the ultimate sacrifice, the King, the High Priest, the Prophet and our brother.

We are allowed to see, throughout the third chapter of Luke, that it is through Mary's father's lineage that Jesus was a descendant of King David. Mary's mother's side most likely provided the

Levite (priestly) lineage. From this lineage then Jesus is considered to be our High Priest.

Saturday

Please use this Space to record any special notes that you thought of while you read this section.

 **Monday**

"The Angels Announcement"

List the dreams for your life that you have had since you were a young child. Are any of them similar to dreams you think Mary may have had for her future?

How would you feel if you had an experience of such magnitude that it rocked your world, just like Mary did?

Have you ever had one? In your Christian life, might you be ignoring or avoiding one, out of fear just as Mary was afraid?

 **Tuesday**

"Mary Ponders The Announcement"

God places within each person who follows after Jesus a dream or a desire to fulfill a mission, to have a role, just as Mary had. [We don't just accept Jesus, and stop…it keeps going.] Like Mary, have you received a calling?

Out of fear, are you resisting responding to that call?

We receive the same promises from God that alleviated Mary' fear. What fears in your life are preventing you from following the dreams and desires that God has placed within you? [List God's promises.]

 # Wednesday

"Mary's Fear For Jesus As The Chief Prophet"

Mary had real fear. She knew her son could be killed for the [religious] truth He would reveal.

Looking back at your dreams, are there any **dreams** that God is calling you to, that if you could know the outcome, you would be willing to die for?

If so, why?

If not, why?

 **Thursday**

"Mary's Fear For Jesus As The King"

God is revealing to Mary a long-term plan for Jesus and for the Kingdom. Jesus lived in a political world. Was his ministry bound or restricted by that political or religious world?

Look through the Gospels and then give some instances where Jesus broke both political and religious rules.

 **Friday**

"God's Birth Announcement"

Mary said, "Here am I, the servant of the Lord; let it be with me according to your word." Then the angel departed from her.

Will you be willing to follow the dream God has place within your heart?

Are you willing to write a prayer to God expressing that willingness and asking for His help in following that dream?

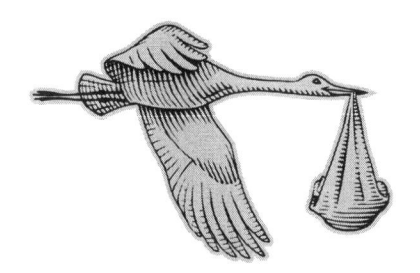

The Third Announcement

Angel's Announcement to Joseph

Matthew 1:20-25

The Christmas Story often overlooks the role that Mary's husband, Joseph, played in the events surrounding the birth of their son, Jesus. We traditionally see this dedicated man, trudging along, leading a donkey laden with his very-pregnant wife and their meager supplies, from Nazareth to the town of Bethlehem. Joseph, an unsung hero, has a life and a story that begin long before the comments made by Matthew.

In many ways for those of us who read a lot of fiction, we are left wondering about many of the details surrounding Mary and Joseph's romance, courtship, and life prior to the sudden arrival of an angel that altered their humble lives.

We could only imagine that at some point in this small village that Joseph became aware of Mary. Most likely, Joseph was not born in Nazareth. We can see through the decree that Caesar sent that all were to go back to the place of their birth. Joseph went back to Bethlehem. I let you romantics begin to fill in the details from there. Just remember that most likely a match maker had to make the final arrangements.

Matthew in his letter to the Israelites leads the reader through a long list of genealogies, just as the reader is about to drift off to sleep he drops on them a burst of world changing information. Out of nowhere he begins to tell the story of the birth of Messiah with; "This is a story of how Jesus came to be...Mary was engaged to be married." The few details Matthew shares up to this point unfold in a staccato burst. To the younger generation who may be reading Matthew's story the tale unfolds in rapid fire, like bullets coming from a machine gun.

Joseph's Dreams Are Shattered

We have all seen the excitement that surrounds a couple as they become engaged. The engagement impacts more than those who are getting married. It affects the whole community. Joseph, after having the marriage arranged, would have had the responsibility of building their new home. Traditionally these were apartments set onto the side of the groom's parent's home.

After his engagement to Mary, Joseph would have gone to work each day as usual—but can you relate with him if he has a hard time keeping his mind on his job? I suspect that the quality of his work went down as he was daydreaming about what he would try to get accomplished on the new home that night.

According to tradition Joseph couldn't get married until the home was complete and acceptable to the father's standards. If it were not up to someone else's standards each newlywed couple might have been willing to live in a tent, since they could be put up in a day. (Don't we all have a problem with waiting for what we want? Look at our society today--we have forgone marriage to simply live with each other.)

If Joseph dreamed the same dreams as you and I did when we were getting ready for marriage, he would have tried to envision his entire life. Joseph would have had dreams about how many children they would have together. He would dream of bringing his boys into the wood shop each day so that he could share not only his trade with them, but also all of the wisdom that he had learned from his father and grandfather.

Joseph I am sure dreamed of the deep intimate relationship he would share with his wife: physically, emotionally, and most important, spiritually. Matthew makes it clear that Joseph was well respected in the community of men, because he was a right living man.

Joseph was living according to all of the rules. The engagement period in the Jewish tradition was just as binding as the marriage only it didn't allow for the couple to live together or to have an intimate relationship with each other. It is here that Joseph's world was shattered. Everything that he dreamed about came to a sudden stop when he finally realized that Mary, his chosen bride, the one that he had been waiting for--was pregnant.

Have you ever received news that caused your heart to simply stop? The kind of news that causes you to become faint from disbelief, news that causes your stomach to want to reject all that you have ever eaten? Every dream that Joseph had came to a sudden stand still. When the news of Mary's pregnancy came to light the men of the town would assume that Joseph was not as righteous as he had claimed to be.

More important to Joseph, since he knew that he had not been intimate with Mary then his bride-to-be must have been disloyal to him. Mary must have found a lover that he knew nothing about. Joseph must have felt betrayed by Mary. This news turned his world upside down.

Can you see the hurt in his eyes as he begins to confront her with his suspicions? Joseph must have expressed his anger and his frustration with her. He also must have had extreme difficulty understanding her explanation. Who had ever claimed before this that some invisible God was the cause of their pregnancy?

Joseph Contemplates Some Sobering Decisions

Joseph had to make a decision now. He had three choices: he could publicly expose Mary as a tramp who had betrayed him; he could quietly have divorce papers drawn up and have her moved away to have the baby in secret; or he could marry her and give the baby his name. It appears he didn't want to do any of these.

Matthew confirms to his readers that Joseph was a compassionate man. Even though his life-long dreams were dashed on the rocks, he took pity on Mary and chose to quietly divorce her and send her away. Mary had already taken one trip down to the town in the Judean hills to see her cousin Elizabeth; maybe she would take Mary in and protect her.

Joseph was facing the trial of his life. In the midst of his trial he chose to show compassion on Mary. This decision didn't come from his mind, but instead from his heart. It is just one of the circumstances that we can see why Joseph was chosen by God to be the stepfather to Jesus. The commitment that Joseph had made to God to be; a loving, caring, compassionate man was deeply engrained into his heart and into his spirit.

Joseph Receives an Announcement

Joseph had made the decision of what to do with Mary before he received his first dream from the angel. Isn't that the same with us, though? We must first exhaust all of our human reasoning before we are given divine insight into the situation.

After Joseph made the difficult decision on what to do regarding Mary he went to bed. This may have been the first good night's rest that Joseph had had since he first found out about her condition. In the middle of the night, most likely as Joseph was entering the deepest part of his sleep, an angel of the Lord appeared to him in a dream. The message was clear: "Joseph, son of David, do not be afraid to take Mary as your wife, for the child conceived in her is from the Holy Spirit. She will bear a son, and you are to name him Jesus, for he will save his people from their sins." Matthew 1:20 &21 (NRSV)

This dream began to turn the nightmare that Joseph had been living into a dream of Hope, Explanation, and finally Exhilaration. This dream began to fill in the gaps that Mary had tried to explain to him over the many conversations that they had. Joseph was finally ready to receive the truth that Mary had been telling him all along. God was good and they were chosen to participate in the coming of the anointed one. They were going to have the responsibility of caring for the Son of God.

Joseph had been taught his entire life to look for the coming of a messiah. Now, here in his room late at night the realization was coming to him that he, Joseph, would play a pivotal role not only in the coming, but also in the raising, of the Jesus. Joseph would have known that Jesus meant "Jehovah is Salvation".

The idea must have scared Joseph, but also exhilarated him, knowing that he was being entrusted to be the stepfather of the Christ child. It was also exhilarating to know that finally after all this time the prophecies of scripture were coming true in real-life time.

Joseph Responds In Obedience

We are not told what happened next, except that he took Mary to be his wife. I think we need to fill in the gap here to fully understand the crises that they were in.

I bet that as soon as Joseph fully comprehended what his dream meant he rushes in to tell his parents that all is well with the world again and he tries to explain to them the change of circumstance. Next, Joseph could be seen running through the little town of Nazareth to wake Mary and tell her the news. He needed to seek her out to ask for his forgiveness in his unwillingness to trust her. He should have known that she was telling him the truth, even though it was so unbelievable.

The joy that must have washed over Mary as her world was being turned right-side up again! She is now loved by the man who she had committed herself to and is also loved by her God who has chosen her to become the mother of Jesus.

I believe that Joseph now put extra time into the building of their new home. If it were me I would drop all else and prepare for the coming of Emmanuel, because God was truly with them. When the time was right Joseph and Mary did become married even though by this time everyone in the town must have known of her condition. If they didn't—they soon would!

Joseph received loud and clear the Birth Announcement that God had sent to him. How about you? When your life receives an unexpected announcement how will you handle it? Will you be able to be as steady as Joseph?

 # Saturday

Please use this Space to record any special notes that you thought of while you read this section.

 **Monday**

"Joseph's Dreams Are Shattered"

Was Joseph, specifically Joseph, a vital part of God's plan in the Christmas Story or just a necessary man in the plan - - necessary but relatively unimportant?

Why do you suppose or think Joseph would have been an appropriate step-father to Jesus? What qualities did God see in Joseph?

Is it possible that God allowed events in Joseph's life that moved him from Bethlehem to Nazareth? Can you see a progression of events in your life leading you from "here to there?"

 # Tuesday

"Joseph Contemplates Some Sobering Decisions"

In your life have you faced a tough decision where all of choices were undesirable, as it appeared to Joseph?

In making that tough decision, did you look outward to with a God-centered response (Love, Compassion, and Generosity) or inward with a self-centered response (Fear, Greed, and Revenge)?

Being a follower of Christ, which do you think you should have used? What scriptures would support your decision making process?

 # Wednesday

"Joseph Receives an Announcement"

"When all else fails, Pray!"

When faced with making a tough decision, do you first exhaust all of your own human reasoning and resources to come up with a solution?

If so, do you then turn to God in prayer, not asking for guidance, but for approval?

What would be the best process you could use in seeking God's will?

 **Thursday**

"Joseph Responds In Obedience"

In the story was Joseph willing to change the course of his first decision because of the dream?

Joseph was willing to go personally to those his decisions had impacted. He went first to his parent to explain his change of plans and then to Mary to seek her forgiveness.

If you have wronged someone would you be willing to follow Joseph example by going to them apologizing and asking for forgiveness?

 **Friday**

"Your Response"

Do you find you expect more of yourself when you are working on a mission for God?

Is this expectation influenced by your relationship with God?

Does this cause you to work differently than you would for worldly missions?

How can you live out daily your mission with a higher expectation for yourself? (May we suggest a deeper relationship with God?)

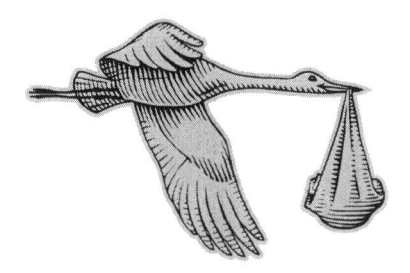

The Fourth Announcement

The Shepherd's Announcement

Luke 2:8-20

The Supreme God of the Universe that created all that is known, seen and unseen, with unlimited powers, continues the pattern of reaching out to those that have been overlooked by society in this, the Fourth Birth Announcement. The Old Testament contains messages for all of humanity concerning the birth of the coming messiah. Mary and Joseph are two simple people living in an out-of-the-way dirty little town. The only thing in their favor is that they have a love of God and live accordingly. In this fourth announcement it seems that this creating God has finally reached to the bottom of the societal barrel.

Shepherds Watch Ceremonial Sheep

Doctor Luke in his record seems to overlook many of the details that today would seem to be significant. He simply introduces the shepherds who were living out in the field watching over their flocks.

The hills around Bethlehem had been a perfect location for raising sheep since little David was out in the fields watching over his father's flocks. The land had rich grass for grazing, and the hills around were dotted with caves: great locations to protect the shepherds in poor weather.

Furthermore, the location of Bethlehem provided an excellent market for the sacrifices at the Temple in Jerusalem. Tradition affords us the knowledge that many of the sheep raised in this area were raised just for this purpose. It was during the special feast days in Israel's religious calendar that thousands of Jewish families would come on a pilgrimage to the holy city. They came from all over the Roman Empire to participate in the festival and to offer up their sacrifices.

Since travel was long and arduous many of those who came to offer their sacrifice would wait until they reached Jerusalem to purchase their sacrificial animal. Here they were able to buy lambs raised just for these occasions. God, in His the instructions to the Israelites, commanded that each of the sheep offered for sacrifice had to be without blemish or defect. This is one of the reasons why the shepherds would have taken such special care when watching over the flocks; the better that the sheep were managed and protected, the fewer blemished ones that then would be found in the flock.

Shepherds Were Ceremonially Unclean

This one simple Birth Announcement from God offers the gift of God's grace on those shepherds. These boys and men were living out in the fields. Their role of taking care of the ceremonial sheep caused them to be away from their families for long periods of time. Their commitment to their job caused them also to become ceremonially unclean in part due to the necessities of the job. They did not have the time to prepare themselves to visit the temple for their own worship.

Because of their occupation shepherds took on the reputation of being very crude and vile men. When they did come into town they were physically dirty and smelled from living so closely with the sheep. It didn't take much for those in town to create rumors of how they lived and how they were known to steal sheep from neighboring flocks. They became associated with those who were the lowest in society.

Yet, it was to these men that the father of the messiah sent an *angel* to give them The Good News. Pretty high treatment for "lowly" sheperds. This is just another way in which God gives each and every one of us a hope for our salvation. It doesn't matter what we have done in our lives. We all fall short of doing it right. Some of us may live in the same conditions, or even worse, than the shepherds out in the field that night. God's grace is given to each one of us for salvation; that is what the Christmas Story is all about.

Shepherds Receive God's Birth Announcement

During the monotony of the night watch the shepherds have a heavenly encounter; one that they would have never expected to have. They knew their position in life and had become accustomed to it.

At some point in your life you may have been outside at night and your eyes became so accustomed to the darkness that you were able to see quite clearly because there was ample light from the moon and stars. I too have experienced this ability. Yet, one night I was out walking when I was momentarily blinded because of a sudden bright light. I couldn't see anything. To be completely honest I was somewhat scared because I couldn't focus. Can you imagine how I felt?

Now, imagine these men staying awake throughout the night to ensure the safety of their flock from natural predators: they were *expecting* danger; they would also be on the alert looking for those who would be sneaking around in the shadows waiting for stragglers that could be stolen. It was in this situation that the blackness of night suddenly burst into the brilliant light of day as the angel of the Lord appeared to proclaim to them.

These brave men were suddenly shaken and terrified. Nothing in their lives would have prepared them to see an angel appear that brought with it the glory of the Lord. Fortunately, this angel didn't leave them in this terrified state for long. The angel said to them, "Do not be afraid, for see--I am bringing you good news of great joy for all the people: to you is born this day in the city of David a Savior, who is the Messiah, the Lord. This will be a sign for you: you will find a child wrapped in bands of cloth and lying in a manger." (Luke 2:10-12 NRSV)

This is the message that every Israelite had been waiting to hear. It had been nearly four thousand years that they had waited for this one single message. They are the first ones to be let in on the secret. These lowly vile men are brought the message of the Good News. Their world will never be the same. They are being invited to one of the most holy moments ever to be witnessed on this side of heaven. These shepherds are invited to come and visit the Jesus, the anointed one.

The Jewish people may have been looking for a political savior, but since the beginning the son of God had been the ultimate sacrifice to break us from the bondage of our sinful character. The bonds of sin will be forever broken. What a Birth Announcement!! These shepherds who were considered to be vile and crude are now on the front row of this event. What does that say to us today? How dare we say that others are too evil for God to save them?

The truth is, just like the shepherds then; you and I today are incapable of being good enough to save ourselves. Despite all our efforts, we are still caught in the grip of sin until we allow the gift God has given to us, his Son Jesus Christ, to become our Savior.

God had promised a redeemer, a savior, a messiah and now here in their midst the wait was over. Look at the words of the angel again. The message was made personal to these shepherds. The angel said "I am bringing you good news of great joy for all the people: to you is born this day in the city of David a Savior, who is the Messiah, the Lord. This will be a sign for you." Even though the message was personally tailored for them it was made available for all of humanity to partake in God's gift of salvation.

We are like the shepherds in that we are caught up in the daily monotonous routines of life. We never know when God will break into this routine with a supernatural event. Like the shepherds we need to be ready to react and to receive the gift given to us. Therefore, be ready when called upon; don't be afraid.

Just as the shepherds were becoming accustomed to the angel speaking to them there were suddenly before them more heavenly host who were praising the God. The message was loud and clear. They were to join in giving praise and honor to the one that was giving the greatest gift of all on this first Christmas.

The shepherds went on to meet Mary and Joseph where they were caring for baby Jesus. They told them of all that had happened to them and Mary hid it away in her heart. The shepherds left that night praising God for all that they had seen and for all that they had heard, but most importantly they left with their hearts transformed. In their heart they would forever sing a new song. It didn't matter what the world thought of them. They were loved by God and were given the grace of eternal forgiveness.

On this Christmas will you be singing with the shepherds the Good News? Has your heart felt the joy that can be found by the one who transforms lives?

Take time today to join the shepherds and the angels in giving praise and honor to the one who sent us the Birth Announcement introducing us to the greatest gift to humanity, Jesus the Messiah.

# Saturday

Please use this Space to record any special notes that you thought of while you read this section.

Monday

"Shepherds Watch Ceremonial Sheep"

By law, the sheep slated for sacrifice had to be without blemish or defect. (See Exodus 12:5; Leviticus 22-23; Numbers 28-29.) Thus, the shepherds in the region of Bethlehem kept close watch over their special sheep—they had a very special duty.

Do you, in your everyday work, consider it (whatever "it" may be) a "special duty," subject to work ethics imposed not by man but by God? Should you? (Philippians 2:13, Ephesians 6:7&8)

How would you feel about your work if you knew that the people who purchased the end product were going to present it in some fashion as a sacrifice to God? Would that change your attitude toward your work?

 **Tuesday**

"Shepherds Were Ceremonially Unclean"

How do you think the shepherds felt about being ceremonially unclean?

How do you think God felt about their condition?

Consider: if it were not for the need of sacrificial sheep for God's people, would have been doing this job at all. Did other people's opinions of their cleanliness (fitness) keep them from doing their job (duty)?

Did their ceremonial uncleanliness keep God from sending a messenger to them and sharing the greatest birth announcement ever?

How do you look at people whose job might render them, in some peoples sight (Perhaps even yours?) "ceremonially unclean"? How do you think God looks at them?

 # Wednesday

"Shepherds Were Ceremonially Unclean"

Have *you* ever felt "ceremonially unclean" due to your job and/or physical appearance?

Has that uncleanliness, either real or imagined, ever kept you from doing what you wanted to, or knew to be right? ("I can't go to that church service/board meeting/dinner committee meeting!!! The baby just dumped strained peas in my hair. My shoes are full of mud--and this shirt! I just won't go—they'll understand.")

Do you feel your occupation or your physical appearance have ever kept *God* from approaching *you*?

What other examples can you find in scripture where God/Jesus approached the "unclean"?

 # Thursday

"Shepherds Receive God's Birth Announcement"

The angel's birth announcement to the shepherds came with no specific orders. Rather, their course of action was implied by the angel's words. "This will be a sign for you; you will find a child wrapped in bands of cloth…" God did not order them to go—but they knew enough to go.

Have you ever put off doing something you felt you should but got out of it by rationalizing? "Well, God hasn't told me I *have* to; therefore it must not be *that* important."

What might you do the next time you find yourself doing this? What, specifically, could you pray and ask God for? Are you willing to do that— are you *going* to do that?

 **Friday**

"Shepherds Receive God's Birth Announcement"

We have used the words lowly, vile, crude, unclean, and dirty to describe the shepherds of Bethlehem, yet God sent not merely a single angle to them with His birth announcement, but threw in a multitude of the heavenly host for good measure. If God so recognized and honored those lowly shepherds then, what type of angels is God sending today to the "shepherds found in our society?

When was the last time *you* approached one of the lowly, the vile, the crude, of your world with the most important Birth Announcement they will ever receive? If not lately--when *will* you act?

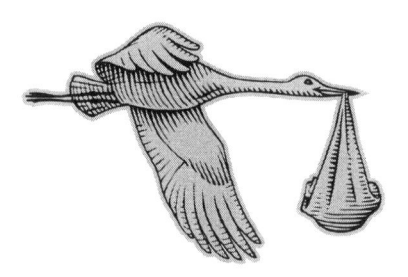

The Fifth Announcement

The Magi's Announcement

Matthew 2:1-11

God's Birth Announcements continue to confound the wise, the rich and the powerful. Each of the invitations given so far has gone to family members that have never been looked upon with great favor: first, to the Israelites, an entire nation of people who had the habit of becoming oppressed; next, to Mary of Nazareth, an ordinary, lowly, no-special-rank-or-privilege teenage girl living in a dirty little town; then to Joseph, a carpenter of no outstanding ability in that same town; and lastly (so far) to a group of dirty heathen hillside shepherds. It would be like inviting to a special celebration that uncle or cousin who always finds a way to embarrass you in front of others. Each of the Birth Announcements has gone to those who have been within the Israelite family. The Old Testament books were directed to the Jewish people. Mary and Joseph fulfilled prophecy by being part of the genealogy of King David. Even the shepherds were most likely descendants of David, since they lived in Bethlehem.

This last Birth Announcement that God provided draws the circle much larger. In fact, we will soon see that God the creator of the universe uses elements within the creation to deliver the last and most important Birth Announcement.

Magi Enter the Kingdom of King Herod

This letter that Matthew is writing was directed to those Jews who were not living in Jerusalem. It was his intent to give them evidence that Jesus was truly their Messiah and this was God's Birth Announcement to them. Matthew begins the Christmas Story with giving them the timeframe just in case they missed it. It was important for Matthew to let them know that King Herod was on the throne.

Even though these Jews lived outside of the holy city, they would have known the terror that just the name of King Herod would evoke in a person. Before we bring in the Magi, let's look a little further into the kingdom into which they are about to enter.

King Herod's reputation extends from this little out-of-the-way Roman province all the way into the inner courts of the Roman Emperor. Before Herod became king he was obsessed with obtaining this as his personal goal or mission and nothing would stop his quest for personal glory.

Herod's father had been murdered due to his role in the murder of Caesar. Herod convinced Mark Antony and Octavian that his father was forced to participate in the murder. It was after Mark Antony marched into Asia that Herod was made the Tetrarch of Galilee. He didn't hold this position for long. Herod's failed to win over the Jews because of his decadent lifestyle. Antigonus capitalized on Herod's failing by taking over his throne. Herod was then forced to return to Rome to save his life and to gather political support.

The Roman Senate then named Herod "King of the Jews." Herod married Mariamne, the niece of Antigonus to help ensure his acceptance by the Jews on his return. He was already married to

Doris and had a son. He had them removed from court so that his throne would be secure.

It took King Herod three years to finally take the rule away from Antigonus. He had him killed and later also killed his new bride Mariamne and the rest of the family to ensure his throne. Herod then proceeded to kill many of the Rabbis and the Pharisees because they were looking for ways to have Herod removed from power.

It was into this environment that the Magi came to pronounce that a new king was born that would be the King of the Jews. This obviously didn't make for a great day when they came knocking on Herod's door so they could worship the new king!

Magi Come From the East

Traditionally it has been difficult to accurately identify who or what the Magi were. It is clearly safe to say that they were not of Jewish decent. This is a critical piece to the salvation puzzle. If they were not Jewish, then the Magi were of a gentile decent. In other words, they were outside of those who were the chosen people of God; very significant.

Let me begin to familiarize you to the purpose of Magi. We believe from all accounts that Magi were from Persia. They executed an important political function for the King of Persia which was to first make him look good to the world. Secondly, they were used by this court to identify new kings and rulers throughout the world. After they saw the signs in the heavens they were sent out as ambassadors of Persia to welcome the new king. We read about them in the Old Testament in both Ezra and Daniel.

Their Latin name "Magi" comes from the ancient Arabic word, "magoi' which has been used to describe those who act in very strange ways. They were captivated by spells, incantations and by the study of astrology. These magoi were known to dress in very bizarre clothes.

Can you imagine the horror of King Herod as these men dressed in wild and strange clothing arrived in a very large caravan coming from the King of Persia? Just as the shock of their mere presence was beginning to wear off they then gave him the news of why they were there and what had brought them: they wanted to know where the newborn king was for they had seen a new star in the sky!

Magi Were Astrologers

God's message of grace and salvation for the gentile is clear with the Birth Announcement going out to the Magi. On Wednesday the devotion will lead us into the study of Deuteronomy and Isaiah where it is clear that astrology and divination are clearly forbidden for the Jews by God. But it is here that the love of God bursts out of heaven for us who are not Jewish.

God provided a Birth Announcement to the Gentiles in the only place they were looking--in the stars. It was for this one special event in history that God, the ruler of both heaven and earth, chose to reveal the message of the anointed messiah to those who were outside of the family. The magi realized that the gentiles were also invited to the celebration of the birth of Jesus.

God is clearly making a statement that the most pagan of the pagans has a place at the family table. It doesn't matter where we come from; what matters is that we come to worship.

Magi Come to Worship

Matthew in this letter is making a strong statement on the purpose of the Magi coming to see the new king. It wasn't just to pay tribute as an ambassador for their king. They came to worship. Matthew use the Greek word proskuneō pronounced *pros-koo-neh'-o* to describe the kind of worship the Magi had. The word that he chose means to kiss like a dog licking his master's hand or to prostrate oneself in a low crouch. Matthew was stating that these weirdly dressed pagans came to adore the new born messiah.

When King Herod found out the purpose of the Magi he called for the chief priests and the scribes. They responded by using the prophet's words from the scriptures to give him the location of the coming messiah. Here is a side note that we will follow-up later in the week. Neither King Herod nor the religious community came along with the Magi to offer their adoration or worship. Instead he had them meet with him in secret to know when the star would have appeared. He knew that if word got out publicly about the coming messiah he would again have to fight for his throne. As Herod sent the Magi on their way he instructed them to return to him with the location so that he could also pay homage. In his heart though we now know that it was his intent to kill the new born king.

Each Christmas season across this country churches put on plays and pageants retelling the birth of Christ. When Magi are presented the focus is on their gifts that are presented to Mary and Jesus. I wonder, though, if their gifts were the most important part of their worship. I believe it was the journey itself. They left Persia firmly rooted in their pagan traditions, but somewhere along the way their hearts were transformed.

Jesus has this effect on us. The Magi represent well the working of the Holy Spirit in our lives. The Magi saw a star which piqued their curiosity. They couldn't control themselves. They had to follow it to its final destination. Our journey to Christ had a similar beginning. We didn't necessarily have a star, but we did have some event or moment in time where we were drawn into a journey of discovery. God in so many different ways provides for us our own personal Birth Announcement. We are invited to celebrate at the foot of the manger. We are drawn into the joy found where the Good News is given.

These Magi may have traveled more than a thousand miles while at the same time the priests who should have been looking for the messiah wouldn't even travel the last six miles with them. How about you--will you travel today to meet the one that was anointed by God the Father?

Epilog to the Magi Story

The focus for many this Christmas will be on the gifts found under the tree. I know that I have become lost in the material game of shopping each year for a good gift, but I wonder if this year I dare to avoid the gift, but instead develop a journey for finding and giving the gift.

If you would give me a little latitude, I would like to end this chapter with a short story. During the Second World War there was a family man who had been sent overseas to the European Theater. He knew that he would not be home for Christmas and his son would need a special gift.

So this father wrote to his son early in the fall to ask what he would want most in this world. Being young and not fully aware of the distance between himself and his father the boy asked for a puppy. Sure enough on Christmas Eve a knock came to the front door. The little boy went to answer it and there in front of him was Santa Clause with a wiggling bag. Santa asked him what he wanted for Christmas and the boy asked for a puppy. Santa reached down into his bag to pull out a special little dog just for the boy.

The next year the father found himself still engaged in the act of war and again wrote home to see what his son would want for Christmas. The return letter from the boy stated that he wanted his father to come home, but his mother said that wouldn't be possible. So instead he asked for a baseball glove and ball so they could play when he did come home.

Christmas Eve came and again there was a knock at the door. The now-growing boy answered the door again to find Santa Clause with a sack of toys. Santa asked the boy what he wanted for Christmas. The lad sure of what was in the bag asked for the glove and ball. Santa pulled out the gift and went on his way.

I am sad to say that this again went on for a third year. The father wrote home to apologize for not being able to make it home again. So in his place he asked the boy what he wanted. This time the boy would only say that he wanted his father to come home. Again the father sent a note saying that it just was not possible and what could he give.

Reluctantly the boy said that he would like to have a new suit so when his father came home they could attend Christmas Eve service together. Again, the boy anticipated the knock on the door that night. With a deep sad heart he went to the door and again saw Santa Clause with a bag full of gifts.

When the usual question came he responded with a soft voice that all he really wanted was his dad, but a suit would be nice. Instead of pulling the suit out of the bag Santa began pulling off his beard. The boy realized that under the white fur and red coat stood his father who had traveled far from the war to be with him on that special night to go to church.

This year it is not the gift of a puppy, a ball and mitt, a suit or gold and diamonds that is valuable. What could be compared to the gift of giving oneself in love? This is what the wise men discovered. They also discovered that God came down from heaven to give himself to you and me through the gift of his son Jesus.

Saturday

Please use this Space to record any special notes that you thought of while you read this section.

 **Monday**

"Magi Enter the Kingdom of King Herod"

Would you consider the quest of today's corporate America for personal gain, glory, and power to be similar to old King Herod's desire?

Does their desire for profit dictate the true meaning of Christmas be submerged in commercialism, just as Herod tried to conceal the message of the Magi?

Have you fallen into their trap of concentrating on the getting and giving of gifts as opposed to appreciating the true meaning the Magi found in Bethlehem?

 # Tuesday

"Magi Come From the East"

The world in essence really doesn't change all that much. How is our world today similar to the world in which the Magi lived where they chased after their own desires prior to seeing the star?

The Magi were pagan representatives for a pagan ruler, yet God opened their eyes and allowed them to see the truth in the one area in which they were looking -- up into the sky. Can you find evidences today where people still find God's Son hidden in a pagan world?

 **Wednesday**

"Magi Were Astrologers"

The Israelites received clear instructions from their God not to use sorcery, divination or astrology. Instead they were to seek wisdom through prophets, scripture and direct revelation from God. On your own search out Deuteronomy 18:10, Joshua 13:22, and Jeremiah 14:14 as just a few examples.

Review the story found in Isaiah 47:5-15. This is a story of how the Israelites turn their back on their Creator to seek after those who stargazers and astrologers in Babylon, the home of the Magi.

Consider; if the Creator was willing to break his own rules to reach the Magi, what is God willing to do today to reach your loved ones?

Thursday

"Magi Come to Worship"

The Magi left home intending to anoint a mortal king; instead they encountered the Christ child that is the Anointed, Everlasting, King of Kings.

The King of all that is seen and unseen loved us so much that he came to the world in the most humble of fashions: as a baby born to humble peasants in a lowly manger. It was this transforming love that the Magi saw and felt so strongly that they fell down in worship.

The question that then comes to each of us today is this: are we willing to fall prostrate in love with this King? What if we were to all come to the manger with that same sense of worshipfulness? Why don't we? What in each of our own lives holds us back from adopting that attitude?

 **Friday**

"Epilogue to the Story"

After all is said and done, do we really want gifts…

Would you agree with me that Christmas
    is more than gifts…

That life is more fulfilling just knowing…

Emmanuel,

    Emmanuel,

        God is with us!

YOUR AUTHOR
STEPHEN CROWELL

For most of Stephen's childhood he lived on what was his grandparent's farm in Western New York. The forests were his playground. At the time he loved the winter months, building ice forts and skiing on the back hill. Now, though, Stephen has a hard time with the winter's cold and snow after living all over the southern states of America.

Stephen was fortunate to have served as youth and young adult pastor under his father in two different Wesleyan Churches. He then was asked to serve a small rural church in Leon, New York which is famous for their Amish community. While serving as a pastor, Stephen completed his Outdoor-Recreation degree from Houghton College. This degree came in handy when Stephen served as a camp director for the United Methodist Church in Pennsylvania.

Currently Stephen is serving as a senior pastor back in Western New York for the United Methodist Church. His passion has been working to develop an emerging church model. Stephen desires to bring people back to the radical message that Jesus taught his disciples. We have a responsibility to be in close intimate fellowship groups that help to support each other through the good and the bad.

Jesus also taught us to have an outward looking focus. Stephen understands that the message of the cross is for those who are marginalized and are sitting on the fringes. He believes that we need to break down all barriers to the foot of the cross. Another area that Stephen feels is important for the community of Christ's followers is to come together regularly to share common meals. It seems that scripture is regularly depicting Jesus eating with friends, relatives, strangers, and most importantly sinners.

Stephen is dedicated to spending any and all spare time traveling with his wife, Kristan, and with any of the kids that desire to come along. They have eight children, one of which is a daughter-in-law. They now use the excuse that the kids live in different parts of the country to visit with them. (Texas, Alaska, Florida)

During the writing of this book, Stephen and Kristan found out that they will become grandparents. What a way to become truly inspired about writing about birth announcements. They are now planning their trip to Texas to welcome Skid.

If this book has helped you with your life's journey Stephen would love to hear from you. If you have a story about how this book has helped you, or changed your life, please share it with him at pastor@konxions.org.

May God bless you on your journey.
Pastor Stephen Crowell

10138834R00061

Made in the USA
Charleston, SC
10 November 2011